People To Buy For:

- [ ] _____
- [ ] _____
- [ ] _____
- [ ] _____
- [ ] _____
- [ ] _____
- [ ] _____
- [ ] _____
- [ ] _____
- [ ] _____
- [ ] _____
- [ ] _____
- [ ] _____
- [ ] _____
- [ ] _____
- [ ] _____
- [ ] _____
- [ ] _____
- [ ] _____
- [ ] _____
- [ ] _____
- [ ] _____
- [ ] _____
- [ ] _____

People To Buy For:

- [ ] _____
- [ ] _____
- [ ] _____
- [ ] _____
- [ ] _____
- [ ] _____
- [ ] _____
- [ ] _____
- [ ] _____
- [ ] _____
- [ ] _____
- [ ] _____
- [ ] _____
- [ ] _____
- [ ] _____
- [ ] _____
- [ ] _____
- [ ] _____
- [ ] _____
- [ ] _____
- [ ] _____
- [ ] _____
- [ ] _____
- [ ] _____
- [ ] _____
- [ ] _____

Name:

_____

Gift Ideas:

_____

_____

_____

_____

Sizes/Notes:

_____

_____

_____

_____

❏ Gift/Gifts Purchased _____

_____

❏ Amount Spent _____

❏ Purchased From _____

❏ On _____

Notes

Name: _____

Gift Ideas:

_____
_____
_____
_____

Sizes/Notes:

_____
_____
_____
_____

❑ Gift/Gifts Purchased _____

❑ Amount Spent _____

❑ Purchased From _____

❑ On _____

Notes

Name:

_____

Gift Ideas:

_____
_____
_____
_____

Sizes/Notes:

_____
_____
_____
_____
_____

- ❏ Gift/Gifts Purchased _____
_____

- ❏ Amount Spent _____

- ❏ Purchased From _____

- ❏ On _____

Notes

Name: _____

Gift Ideas:

_____
_____
_____
_____

Sizes/Notes:

_____
_____
_____
_____

❏ Gift/Gifts Purchased _____

_____

❏ Amount Spent _____

❏ Purchased From _____

❏ On _____

Notes

Name:

_____

Gift Ideas:

_____

_____

_____

_____

Sizes/Notes:

_____

_____

_____

_____

❑ Gift/Gifts Purchased _____

_____

❑ Amount Spent _____

❑ Purchased From _____

❑ On _____

Notes

Name:

_____

Gift Ideas:

_____

_____

_____

_____

Sizes/Notes:

_____

_____

_____

_____

❑ Gift/Gifts Purchased _____

_____

❑ Amount Spent _____

❑ Purchased From _____

❑ On _____

Notes

Name:

_____

Gift Ideas:

_____

_____

_____

_____

Sizes/Notes:

_____

_____

_____

_____

❑ Gift/Gifts Purchased _____

_____

❑ Amount Spent _____

❑ Purchased From _____

❑ On _____

Notes

Name:

_____

Gift Ideas:

_____

_____

_____

_____

Sizes/Notes:

_____

_____

_____

_____

_____

❏ Gift/Gifts Purchased _____

_____

❏ Amount Spent _____

❏ Purchased From _____

❏ On _____

Notes

Name:

_____

Gift Ideas:

_____
_____
_____
_____

Sizes/Notes:

_____
_____
_____
_____
_____

- ❑ Gift/Gifts Purchased _____
  _____
- ❑ Amount Spent _____
- ❑ Purchased From _____
- ❑ On _____

Notes

Name:

_____

Gift Ideas:

_____

_____

_____

_____

Sizes/Notes:

_____

_____

_____

_____

- ❑ Gift/Gifts Purchased _____

  _____

- ❑ Amount Spent _____

- ❑ Purchased From _____

- ❑ On _____

Notes

Name:

_____

Gift Ideas:

_____
_____
_____
_____

Sizes/Notes:

_____
_____
_____
_____

❑ Gift/Gifts Purchased _____

❑ Amount Spent _____

❑ Purchased From _____

❑ On _____

Notes

Name:
_____

Gift Ideas:

_____
_____
_____
_____

Sizes/Notes:

_____
_____
_____
_____
_____

❑ Gift/Gifts Purchased _____

_____

❑ Amount Spent _____

❑ Purchased From _____

❑ On _____

Notes

Name:

_____

Gift Ideas:

_____

_____

_____

_____

Sizes/Notes:

_____

_____

_____

_____

_____

☐ Gift/Gifts Purchased _____

_____

☐ Amount Spent _____

☐ Purchased From _____

☐ On _____

Notes

Name: _____

Gift Ideas:

_____

_____

_____

_____

Sizes/Notes:

_____

_____

_____

_____

❑ Gift/Gifts Purchased _____

_____

❑ Amount Spent _____

❑ Purchased From _____

❑ On _____

Notes

Name:

_____

Gift Ideas:

_____

_____

_____

_____

Sizes/Notes:

_____

_____

_____

_____

_____

❏ Gift/Gifts Purchased _____

_____

❏ Amount Spent _____

❏ Purchased From _____

❏ On _____

Notes

Name:

_____

Gift Ideas:

_____
_____
_____
_____

Sizes/Notes:

_____
_____
_____
_____
_____

- ☐ Gift/Gifts Purchased _____
_____

- ☐ Amount Spent _____

- ☐ Purchased From _____

- ☐ On _____

Notes

Name: _____

Gift Ideas:

_____
_____
_____
_____

Sizes/Notes:

_____
_____
_____
_____
_____

☐ Gift/Gifts Purchased _____
_____

☐ Amount Spent _____

☐ Purchased From _____

☐ On _____

Notes

Name: _____

Gift Ideas:

_____
_____
_____
_____

Sizes/Notes:

_____
_____
_____
_____
_____

❏ Gift/Gifts Purchased _____

_____

❏ Amount Spent _____

❏ Purchased From _____

❏ On _____

Notes

Name:

_____

Gift Ideas:

_____
_____
_____
_____

Sizes/Notes:

_____
_____
_____
_____
_____

- ❏ Gift/Gifts Purchased _____
  _____
- ❏ Amount Spent _____
- ❏ Purchased From _____
- ❏ On _____

Notes

Name:

_____

Gift Ideas:

_____
_____
_____
_____

Sizes/Notes:

_____
_____
_____
_____

❏ Gift/Gifts Purchased _____

❏ Amount Spent _____

❏ Purchased From _____

❏ On _____

Notes

Name: _____

Gift Ideas:

_____
_____
_____
_____

Sizes/Notes:

_____
_____
_____
_____
_____

❏ Gift/Gifts Purchased _____

_____

❏ Amount Spent _____

❏ Purchased From _____

❏ On _____

Notes

Name:
_____

Gift Ideas:

_____
_____
_____
_____

Sizes/Notes:

_____
_____
_____
_____

❑ Gift/Gifts Purchased _____

_____

❑ Amount Spent _____

❑ Purchased From _____

❑ On _____

Notes

Name: _____

Gift Ideas:

_____
_____
_____
_____

Sizes/Notes:

_____
_____
_____
_____

❑ Gift/Gifts Purchased _____

_____

❑ Amount Spent _____

❑ Purchased From _____

❑ On _____

Notes

Name:

_____

Gift Ideas:

_____
_____
_____
_____

Sizes/Notes:

_____
_____
_____
_____
_____

- ❏ Gift/Gifts Purchased _____
_____

- ❏ Amount Spent _____

- ❏ Purchased From _____

- ❏ On _____

Notes

Name:

_____

Gift Ideas:

_____
_____
_____
_____

Sizes/Notes:

_____
_____
_____
_____
_____

- ❏ Gift/Gifts Purchased _____

_____

- ❏ Amount Spent _____
- ❏ Purchased From _____
- ❏ On _____

Notes

Name:

_____

Gift Ideas:

_____
_____
_____
_____

Sizes/Notes:

_____
_____
_____
_____
_____

☐ Gift/Gifts Purchased _____

_____

☐ Amount Spent _____

☐ Purchased From _____

☐ On _____

Notes

Name:

Gift Ideas:

_____
_____
_____
_____

Sizes/Notes:

_____
_____
_____
_____
_____

- ❏ Gift/Gifts Purchased _____

_____

- ❏ Amount Spent _____

- ❏ Purchased From _____

- ❏ On _____

Notes

Name:

_____

Gift Ideas:

_____
_____
_____
_____

Sizes/Notes:

_____
_____
_____
_____
_____

☐ Gift/Gifts Purchased _____

_____

☐ Amount Spent _____

☐ Purchased From _____

☐ On _____

Notes

Name:

Gift Ideas:

_____

_____

_____

_____

Sizes/Notes:

_____

_____

_____

_____

_____

☐ Gift/Gifts Purchased _____

_____

☐ Amount Spent _____

☐ Purchased From _____

☐ On _____

Notes

Name:

Gift Ideas:

_____
_____
_____
_____

Sizes/Notes:

_____
_____
_____
_____
_____

❑ Gift/Gifts Purchased _____

_____

❑ Amount Spent _____

❑ Purchased From _____

❑ On _____

Notes

Name:

Gift Ideas:

_____

_____

_____

_____

Sizes/Notes:

_____

_____

_____

_____

_____

- ☐ Gift/Gifts Purchased _____

_____

- ☐ Amount Spent _____
- ☐ Purchased From _____
- ☐ On _____

Notes

Name:
_____

Gift Ideas:

_____
_____
_____
_____

Sizes/Notes:

_____
_____
_____
_____

❑ Gift/Gifts Purchased _____
_____

❑ Amount Spent _____

❑ Purchased From _____

❑ On _____

Notes

Name:

_____

Gift Ideas:

_____
_____
_____
_____

Sizes/Notes:

_____
_____
_____
_____
_____

❏ Gift/Gifts Purchased _____

_____

❏ Amount Spent _____

❏ Purchased From _____

❏ On _____

Notes

Name:
_____

Gift Ideas:

_____
_____
_____
_____

Sizes/Notes:

_____
_____
_____
_____
_____

❏ Gift/Gifts Purchased _____

_____

❏ Amount Spent _____

❏ Purchased From _____

❏ On _____

Notes

Name:
_____

Gift Ideas:
_____
_____
_____
_____

Sizes/Notes:
_____
_____
_____
_____
_____

❏ Gift/Gifts Purchased _____
_____

❏ Amount Spent _____

❏ Purchased From _____

❏ On _____

Notes

Name:

_____

Gift Ideas:

_____
_____
_____
_____

Sizes/Notes:

_____
_____
_____
_____
_____

- ☐ Gift/Gifts Purchased _____

_____

- ☐ Amount Spent _____
- ☐ Purchased From _____
- ☐ On _____

Notes

Name:

_____

Gift Ideas:

_____

_____

_____

_____

Sizes/Notes:

_____

_____

_____

_____

_____

❑ Gift/Gifts Purchased _____

_____

❑ Amount Spent _____

❑ Purchased From _____

❑ On _____

Notes

Name:

_____

Gift Ideas:

_____
_____
_____
_____

Sizes/Notes:

_____
_____
_____
_____
_____

❏ Gift/Gifts Purchased _____

_____

❏ Amount Spent _____

❏ Purchased From _____

❏ On _____

Notes

Name:

_____

Gift Ideas:

_____

_____

_____

_____

Sizes/Notes:

_____

_____

_____

_____

_____

❏ Gift/Gifts Purchased _____

_____

❏ Amount Spent _____

❏ Purchased From _____

❏ On _____

Notes

Name:

_____

Gift Ideas:

_____
_____
_____
_____

Sizes/Notes:

_____
_____
_____
_____

- ☐ Gift/Gifts Purchased _____

_____

- ☐ Amount Spent _____
- ☐ Purchased From _____
- ☐ On _____

Notes

Name: _____

Gift Ideas:

_____
_____
_____
_____

Sizes/Notes:

_____
_____
_____
_____
_____

☐ Gift/Gifts Purchased _____

_____

☐ Amount Spent _____

☐ Purchased From _____

☐ On _____

Notes

Name:
_____

Gift Ideas:

_____
_____
_____
_____

Sizes/Notes:

_____
_____
_____
_____
_____

❏ Gift/Gifts Purchased _____

_____

❏ Amount Spent _____

❏ Purchased From _____

❏ On _____

Notes

Name:

Gift Ideas:

_____
_____
_____
_____
_____

Sizes/Notes:

_____
_____
_____
_____
_____

❑ Gift/Gifts Purchased _____
_____

❑ Amount Spent _____

❑ Purchased From _____

❑ On _____

Notes

Name:
_____

Gift Ideas:
_____
_____
_____
_____

Sizes/Notes:
_____
_____
_____
_____
_____

❏ Gift/Gifts Purchased _____
_____

❏ Amount Spent _____

❏ Purchased From _____

❏ On _____

Notes

Name:

_____

Gift Ideas:

_____
_____
_____
_____

Sizes/Notes:

_____
_____
_____
_____
_____

- ❏ Gift/Gifts Purchased _____

  _____

- ❏ Amount Spent _____

- ❏ Purchased From _____

- ❏ On _____

Notes

Name:

_____

Gift Ideas:

_____
_____
_____
_____

Sizes/Notes:

_____
_____
_____
_____
_____

❑ Gift/Gifts Purchased _____
_____

❑ Amount Spent _____

❑ Purchased From _____

❑ On _____

Notes

Name:

Gift Ideas:

_____

_____

_____

_____

Sizes/Notes:

_____

_____

_____

_____

_____

☐ Gift/Gifts Purchased _____

☐ Amount Spent _____

☐ Purchased From _____

☐ On _____

Notes

Name:

_____

Gift Ideas:

_____

_____

_____

_____

Sizes/Notes:

_____

_____

_____

_____

_____

❏ Gift/Gifts Purchased _____

_____

❏ Amount Spent _____

❏ Purchased From _____

❏ On _____

Notes

Name:

_____

Gift Ideas:

_____

_____

_____

_____

Sizes/Notes:

_____

_____

_____

_____

_____

❏ Gift/Gifts Purchased _____

_____

❏ Amount Spent _____

❏ Purchased From _____

❏ On _____

Notes

Name:

_____

Gift Ideas:

_____
_____
_____
_____

Sizes/Notes:

_____
_____
_____
_____
_____

☐ Gift/Gifts Purchased _____

_____

☐ Amount Spent _____

☐ Purchased From _____

☐ On _____

Notes

Name:

_____

Gift Ideas:

_____
_____
_____
_____

Sizes/Notes:

_____
_____
_____
_____
_____

❑ Gift/Gifts Purchased _____

_____

❑ Amount Spent _____

❑ Purchased From _____

❑ On _____

Notes

Name:

_____

Gift Ideas:

_____
_____
_____
_____

Sizes/Notes:

_____
_____
_____
_____
_____

❑ Gift/Gifts Purchased _____

_____

❑ Amount Spent _____

❑ Purchased From _____

❑ On _____

Notes

Name:

Gift Ideas:

_____

_____

_____

_____

Sizes/Notes:

_____

_____

_____

_____

❑ Gift/Gifts Purchased _____

_____

❑ Amount Spent _____

❑ Purchased From _____

❑ On _____

Notes

www.ingramcontent.com/pod-product-compliance
Lightning Source LLC
LaVergne TN
LVHW021549080125
800829LV00008B/461